Armstrong

by Grace Franklin

LangSyne

PUBLISHING

WRITING *to* REMEMBER

Lang**Syne**

PUBLISHING

WRITING *to* REMEMBER

79 Main Street, Newtongrange,
Midlothian EH22 4NA
Tel: 0131 344 0414   Fax: 0845 075 6085
E-mail: info@lang-syne.co.uk
www.langsyneshop.co.uk

Design by Dorothy Meikle
Printed by Printwell Ltd
© Lang Syne Publishers Ltd 2017

ISBN 978-1-85217-064-6

Armstrong

SEPT NAMES INCLUDE:
No proven septs but Kinmont
is a likely contender.

Armstrong

MOTTO:
Invictus maneo
(I remain unvanquished).

PLANT BADGE:
Thyme.

TERRITORY:
Liddesdale, Roxburghshire.
The edge of the Southern Uplands
around Liddel Water.

Chapter one:

The origins of the clan system

by Rennie McOwan

**The original Scottish clans of the Highlands
and the great families of the Lowlands and
Borders were gatherings of families, relatives,
allies and neighbours for mutual protection
against rivals or invaders.**

Scotland experienced invasion from the
Vikings, the Romans and English armies from the
south. The Norman invasion of what is now
England also had an influence on land-holding in
Scotland. Some of these invaders stayed on and in
time became 'Scottish'.

The word clan derives from the Gaelic
language term 'clann', meaning children, and it
was first used many centuries ago as communities
were formed around tribal lands in glens and
mountain fastnesses.

The format of clans changed over the centuries, but at its best the chief and his family held the land on behalf of all, like trustees, and the ordinary clansmen and women believed they had a blood relationship with the founder of their clan.

There were two way duties and obligations. An inadequate chief could be deposed and replaced by someone of greater ability.

Clan people had an immense pride in race. Their relationship with the chief was like adult children to a father and they had a real dignity.

The concept of clanship is very old and a more feudal notion of authority gradually crept in

Pictland, for instance, was divided into seven principalities ruled by feudal leaders who were the strongest and most charismatic leaders of their particular groups.

By the sixth century the 'British' kingdoms of Strathclyde, Lothian and Celtic Dalriad (Argyll) had emerged and Scotland, as one nation began to take shape in the time of King Kennet MacAlpin.

Some chiefs claimed descent from

ancient kings which may not have been accurate in every case.

By the twelfth and thirteenth centuries the clans and families were more strongly brought under the central control of Scottish monarchs.

Lands were awarded and administered more and more under royal favour, yet the power of the area clan chiefs was still very great.

The long wars to ensure Scotland's independence against the expansionist ideas of English monarchs extended the influence of some clans and reduced the lands of others.

Those who supported Scotland's greatest king, Robert the Bruce, were awarded the territories of the families who had opposed his claim to the Scottish throne.

In the Scottish Borders country – the notorious Debatable Lands – the great families built up a ferocious reputation for providing warlike men accustomed to raiding into England and occasionally fighting one another.

Chiefs had the power to dispense justice and to confiscate lands and clan warfare produced

a society where martial virtues – courage, hardiness
tenacity – were greatly admired.

Gradually the relationship between the
clans and the Crown became strained as Scottish
monarchs became more orientated to life in the
Lowlands and, on occasion, towards England.

The Highland clans spoke a different
language, Gaelic, whereas the language of
Lowland Scotland and the court was Scots and in
more modern times, English.

Highlanders dressed differently, had
different customs, and their wild mountain land
sometimes seemed almost foreign to people living
in the Lowlands.

It must be emphasised that Gaelic culture
was very rich and story-telling, poetry, piping, the
clarsach (harp) and other music all flourished and
were greatly respected.

Highland culture was different from othe
parts of Scotland but it was not inferior or les
sophisticated.

Central Government, whether in Londc
or Edinburgh, sometimes saw the Gaelic clans a

*"The spirit of the clan means much
to thousands of people"*

a challenge to their authority and some sent
expeditions into the Highlands and west to crush
the power of the Lords of the Isles.

Nevertheless, when the eighteenth century
Jacobite Risings came along the cause of the
Stuarts was mainly supported by Highland clans.

The word Jacobite comes from the Latin
for James – Jacobus. The Jacobites wanted to
restore the exiled Stuarts to the throne of Britain.

The monarchies of Scotland and England
became one in 1603 when King James VI of
Scotland (1st of England) gained the English
throne after Queen Elizabeth died.

The Union of Parliaments of Scotland and
England, the Treaty of Union, took place in 1707.

Some Highland clans, of course, and
Lowland families opposed the Jacobites and
supported the incoming Hanoverians.

After the Jacobite cause finally went down
at Culloden in 1746 a kind of ethnic cleansing took
place. The power of the chiefs was curtailed.
Tartan and the pipes were banned in law.

Many emigrated, some because they

wanted to, some because they were evicted by force. In addition, many Highlanders left for the cities of the south to seek work.

Many of the clan lands became home to sheep and deer shooting estates.

But the warlike traditions of the clans and the great Lowland and Border families lived on, with their descendants fighting bravely for freedom in two world wars.

Remember the men from whence you came, says the Gaelic proverb, and to that could be added the role of many heroic women.

The spirit of the clan, of having roots, whether Highland or Lowland, means much to thousands of people.

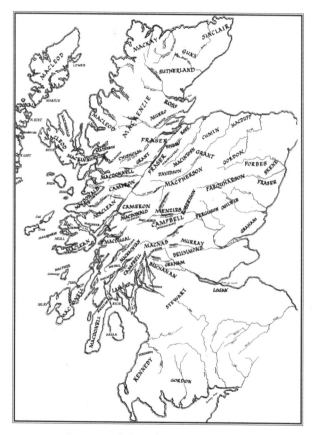

A map of the clans' homelands

Chapter two:

Saving the King

As the name suggests, the Armstrong Clan are people renowned for their strength. Traditionally armour bearers to the King of Scots, this serious post virtually meant the King's life was in their hands.

It was an act of bravery and strength in the middle of a hard fought battle which confirmed the Armstrong name and established the Clan.

The King's horse had been killed and he was trapped beneath the animal's dead weight. Seeing this, the King's armour bearer lifted the horse to free his King and so save his life. Another version of the legend says he grabbed the King by the thigh and swung him onto the back of his own steed to escape.

However it happened, the King was duly grateful, praised his armour bearer for saving his life and set the name Armstrong in the history books for ever. His thank you gift was a little matter of spectacular rolling hills and dales in Liddesdale valley, Roxburghshire. That's where the Clan flourished, particularly in the 13th century.

Ten clan chiefs have been counted but the last one died in 1610. After that the clan scattered abroad. But in those intervening centuries the Armstrongs were famous in that Borders area as reivers or raiders.

Contentious territory, the great swaths of land between the Rivers Esk and Sark changed hands between England and Scotland at least 13 times in those blood-thirsty days. As part of the frequent raids to steal cattle, and horses, (occasionally women too) the surrounding houses and crops would be torched. After cattle had been stolen the owner had 24 hours to go in hot pursuit. He did this with a burning peat at the tip of his lance to warn everyone what he was about and to clear out of his road. If he was successful and found his livestock in that time, he was supposed to be able to reclaim it without question. But if more than 24 hours had elapsed, it was a case of finder is keeper and he'd have to fight for the return of his property.

Reiving, or raiding of this kind was the business of the day. And the Armstrongs with their great allies the Elliots, were foremost among the Border Reivers. They ran, what might be called today, protection rackets – pay us and we'll protect you and your property. But they were men of honour and woe betide the man who didn't keep his word.

Life for the ordinary Reiver on raiding forays was rough. Shelter was a fairly flimsy affair of bowed trees and pine branches which could be created as quickly as it would invariably, be destroyed. Firing of the land was common-place and a natural event in the course of a raid. The Thieves' Road and the Captain's Road are still used but nowadays it will be walkers on the Southern Uplands Way who enjoy the majesty of the fine hill tracks. In days gone by these were the Drove Roads where the herds of sheep and cattle were brought to markets or where the Reivers clandestinely led their newly acquired stock.

When Castleton was burned to the ground it was re-created three or four miles away and re-named Newcastleton. The place can still be found today, but in a more substantial form, at the edge of the Cheviot Hills.

Always war-like, the Armstrongs could be described as mercenaries. In one infamous battle when they had been hired by an English Baron, they discovered with horror, they were fighting their own clansmen on the opposing side. The Armstrongs on the English side immediately stripped off their St George's Cross garb and joined their kin on the other side to defeat the army they'd originally been hired by. This gave rise to the acidic comment that the Armstrongs are 'bonnie fechters if they kent which side they were on'.

They so lived up to their reputation as unruly that a Keeper of Liddesdale was appointed by the monarch to attempt to keep them in check. Things reached a degree of settlement in 1552 when the French Ambassador was chosen as the 'referee' to supervise the division of the bitterly disputed territories between the River Sark and Esk. This brought some peace to the area.

But not all Armstrongs were of a quarrelsome nature. Gilbert Armstrong was Steward of the Household to King David III around 1363 so knew how to keep the peace in the royal chambers. He eventually became Scotland's ambassador to England which enabled him to play a part in establishing diplomatic relations between the two nations.

Alexander was the name of the first clan chief. He held sway in Mangerton, the family seat, at the end of the 13th century. At that time the Borders was roughly divided into three parts – the West March, the Middle March and the East March. Each March was jealously guarded territory. Most of the Armstrongs lived in the west end of the Middle March towards the south of the village of Castleton. Their long time friends and fighting companions the Elliots, generally inhabited the areas to the north.

To this day, the Riding of the Marches is a tradition which reflects those troubled times when marking out, establishing, keeping or re-taking territory was so important.

At the height of the Armstong power, the Lairds of Mangerton presided over as many as 80 or 90 sturdy, stone built, tower houses and an estimated 250 farms in their hard-won lands. They were guardians of all the clans who lived there, including the fighting men, the Reivers who with their families, had their lives disrupted by the frequent and violent raids, fire and destruction.

Naturally, covetous eyes would be cast over such extensive land and power.

Chapter three:

Betrayal!

The first written account of an Armstrong is, as one might expect, in the court reports of Carlisle. In the 13th century this was a key stronghold and border town of great strategic importance. As far back as 1018 it was part of Cumbria which together with Strathclyde and Lothian were all under the Scottish Crown. Duncan Irving of Eskdale was Governor of Cumbria and had his official residence in Carlisle. But his private retreat was in Upper Eskdale in Dumfriesshire. So commuters are not confined to the 20th century.

Those Carlisle law records of 1235 note an Adam Armstrong of Cumberland was pardoned for 'causing the death of another man.' The circumstances are not recorded but the fact that he was pardoned showed the crime was considered to have been accidental otherwise he would have been hung.

Only a generation later in 1281 a John Armstrong is stated to have been killed by a James de Multon. This was serious as they were both high ranking nobles. The diplomatic wheeling and dealing required King Alexander III of Scotland to obtain a pardon from his brother-in-law King Edward I of England. This makes it clear that John Armstrong was Scottish and of high rank if his King was concerned in the matter.

It is worth remembering that some of the Normans who landed with William the Conqueror and were so successful in Sussex in 1066, moved north. In time, some settled in the Borders and even further into Scotland. They included another nobleman called Robert de Brus. So James de Multon's pedigree can be deduced.

The unfortunate, dead, John Armstrong was the father of Alexander the first Chief of the clan.

In Borders terms membership of a clan was strictly kinship, showing descent through the blood line. In Highland terms, clan membership was used as politically required and changed as a matter of convenience or expediency.

'When you strike my brother, you strike me.' Could well have been the motto of the Armstrongs. They stuck together and lived and died together. Some of the incidents in their gory records have been immortalised in folk songs which are still heard today.

None was as powerful or as shocking – even in those fighting times as the shameful murder of Johnie Armstrong of Gilnockie.

It was in 1530 when what became known as a 'loving letter' was sent by the King James V of Scotland to all nobles. He said he was making a grand hunting tour of the country and invited local nobles at each stopping point to join him in the hunt. The invitation was exceptional and Johnie accepted with good grace. Whatever feuds he might have had with his King he got ready to welcome the royal entourage to his tower home.

Venison was prepared, the place made ready to receive the Royal guest and Johnie and his men road out – as was courtesy – to meet the King at a suitable point called Carlinrigg and ride with them the last miles to Johnie's base.

Chapter four:

Great escape

**That valley where the two Waters meet is
as beautiful as it was the day Johnie set out.
The spectacular view of the confluence of
from an original Telford Bridge. At points like
this where water runs fast, the Clan marriage
ceremony would take place.**

The man and the woman would stretch
across and clasp hands. This signalled a one year
contract as a couple. At the end of the year they
could return and re-seal the deal for life or to call
the whole thing off.

Water and marshy lands were second
nature to the Armstrongs. They were experts in
such terrain – taking short cuts with herds of
cattle at night makes you sure footed. And the
natural affinity with, and great dependence on, a
good horse made them wiley foes.

At Tarras Moss a marshy area where the
clan lived, 400 were surrounded on one famous

occasion by a strong band of English raiders. The English opponents thought they had nothing to do but starve the Armstrongs out. But they hadn't reckoned on the native knowledge of the Armstrongs.

After some weeks, the clan took pity on their hungry foes and sent out some beasts for the English to slaughter. The unexpectedly long vigil they found they had undertaken meant they were running out of food. When the English had eaten well and slumped into a satisfied sleep, the entire clan simply picked their way out by the light of the moon, using the obscure pathways through the marshes which they, their horses and their sure footed cattle knew intimately.

It is alleged that such skill on wetlands points to Armstrongs being the perpetrators of a most unusual crime. A certain Lord Durie was kidnapped from the sands of Musselburgh while he was out riding one morning at early tide. The law lord was hearing a case against Lord Traquair. Lord Traquair anticipated losing. According to legend, Lord Traquair called in a favour from the clan and got them to lift the law lord and spirit him away for two or three months and keep him in one of the marshy hide-aways or perhaps Annandale Tower. The law lord came to no harm and was returned, on his horse, to the very sands from which he had been snatched.

The Armstrong who is supposed to have led that little expedition was Christie's Will. He was ambushed by Cromwell's men while on a bridge spanning the River Eden. Alerted by the sound of horses hooves coming from both ends of the bridge, he took a dive into the river and swam away. As with all nice legends of this type he is alleged to have shot at least one soldier before his powder got wet.

This William was the son of Christopher Armstrong of Barngleish. The same Christopher who's father Johnie had been hanged by King James V.

The family later lived in Langholm Castle. Christie's Will fought King Charles I in Ireland and had land in Fermanagh and Ulster around 1615-20. He fought in Europe in Njimegen in Holland and is thought to have fought under

Buccleuch in the clearances of the Borders. A professional soldier, he was killed in battle.

With the close alliance of the Armstrongs and the Elliots it was not surprising that his wife was a Margaret Elliot. They had seven sons. Sir Thomas the elder became a Quartermaster General. Edward had land at Terwinney, Alexander settled in Carrick Mackeegan. Only the names are known of Simon and Robert. John was of Longfield and David was of Kirtletown in Dumfriesshire.

Surnames were not common – a man took his identity from the place he stayed or from his parent's attributes. So the man known as Kinmont Willie was William Armstrong who lived at Kinmont. His famous escapade allows the names Kinmont to be the only likely recognised, sept of the clan.

On his way home on a day of truce – when all arguments and debts were settled in a formalised way and at a recognised place according to strict rules – Willie was captured by the English on the Scottish side of the river Esk. He was chased four miles before being overtaken and incarcerated in

Carlisle Castle. This act was a scandalous breach of the truce etiquette. No man should be challenged on truce days except in the accepted places.

But he didn't wait long in the dungeon, chained to the wall.

His clan met at a horse race in Langholm later in 1596. They made plans to rescue him under cover of the social occasion. A band of 24, which included some faithful Elliots, went to Carlisle Castle at dead of night. They surprised the guards, overran the garrison, unchained Willie from his fetters and all escaped through the postern gate, a side door. They raced off across the border to the safety of their homes in Scotland. Such a brazen raid was an affront to the military in charge of security of the Castle. Queen Elizabeth of England was not amused. Carlisle, after all, played a vital role in defending that country's territory. If a major garrison was caught napping, where would it end?

Of course, in time the feuding did end and the need for the clan as a disciplined group vanished with it.

Chapter five:

Pride and honesty

The reign of the ten Clan chiefs spanned more than 300 years of turbulent history. It started in the Golden Age of Scots King Alexander III around 1275 and ended with the death of the tenth chief, the laird of Mangerton in 1610.

Along with Elliot, Nixon and Crozer the Armstrongs were named as clans inhabiting the Middle March of the Borders in an early Act of the Scottish Parliament. In another Act – of 1672 a David Armstrong of Park was registered to bear arms. Old ways don't die, they adapt into new situations.

Such history lives on and is preserved by those who carry that proud name.

The first Clan gathering for 400 years took place at Tourneyholm in Flattdale in England in 1979. This was the place where the Wardens of England and Scotland met in olden times to settle bills from the cross-border raids. While these